# COCKATIELS

## Belinda Ogle

Heinemann Library
Chicago, Illinois

*E S*

© 2004 Reed Educational & Professional Publishing

Published by Heinemann Library,

an imprint of Reed Educational & Professional Publishing,

Chicago, Illinois


Customer Service  888-454-2279

Visit our website at www.heinemannlibrary.com

Designed by Ron Kamen and Celia Floyd

Photo research by Rebecca Sodergren

Originated by Dot Gradiations Limited

Printed in China by WKT Company Limited


08 07 06 05 04

10 9 8 7 6 5 4 3 2 1

**Library of Congress Cataloging-in-Publication Data**

Ogle, Belinda.

   Cockatiels / Belinda Ogle.

      p. cm. -- (Keeping unusual pets)

Contents: What is a cockatiel -- Cockatiels in the wild -- Is a cockatiel for you? -- What do I need? -- Caring for your cockatiel -- Can we make friends? -- Fun time together -- Keeping your Cockatiel healthy -- Some health problems -- When a Cocktatiel dies -- Keeping a record.

   ISBN 1-4034-0824-6

   1. Cockatiel--Juvenile literature. [1. Cockatiel. 2. Pets.]  I. Title. II. Series.

   SF473.C6O44 2004

   636.6'8656--dc22

                                                2003015530

**Acknowledgements**

The publishers would like to thank the following for permission to reproduce photographs:

Ardea/D & M Trounson: p. 16 (top); Ardea/Jean-Paul Ferrero: p. 9 (top); Ardea/John Daniels: p. 6 (top); Corbis/Eric and David Hosking: p. 7; FLPA: p. 8; FLPA/J&P Wegner: p. 18; Maria Joannou: p. 43; NHPA/Ernie Janes: pp. 17, 6 (bottom); Oxford Scientific Films/Steve Turner: p. 5; Oxford Scientific Films/Austin J Stevens: p. 9 (bottom); Tudor Photography: pp. 10, 11 (top), 11 (bottom), 12, 13, 14, 15 (top), 15 (bottom), 16 (bottom), 19, 20, 21 (top), 21 (bottom), 22, 23 (top), 23 (bottom), 24, 25 (top), 25 (bottom), 26, 27 (top), 27 (bottom), 28, 29 (top), 29 (bottom), 30, 31, 32, 33 (top), 33 (bottom), 34, 35, 36 (top), 36 (bottom), 37, 38, 39 (top), 39 (bottom), 40, 41 (top), 41 (bottom), 44, 45 (top), 45 (bottom).


Cover photograph of the cockatiel, reproduced with permission of Tudor Photography.

# Contents

What Is a Cockatiel?. . . . . . . . . . . . . . . . . . . . . . . . 4

Cockatiels in the Wild. . . . . . . . . . . . . . . . . . . . . 8

Is a Cockatiel for You? . . . . . . . . . . . . . . . . . 10

Choosing a Cockatiel . . . . . . . . . . . . . . . . . . 14

What Do I Need? . . . . . . . . . . . . . . . . . . . . . . 20

Caring for Your Cockatiel . . . . . . . . . . . . . . . 26

Can We Make Friends?. . . . . . . . . . . . . . . . . . 32

Fun Time Together. . . . . . . . . . . . . . . . . . . . . 34

Keeping Your Cockatiel Healthy . . . . . . . . . . . 38

Some Health Problems. . . . . . . . . . . . . . . . . . 40

When a Cockatiel Dies. . . . . . . . . . . . . . . . . . 42

Keeping a Record . . . . . . . . . . . . . . . . . . . . . 44

*Glossary*. . . . . . . . . . . . . . . . . . . . . . . . . . . . 46

*Further Reading*. . . . . . . . . . . . . . . . . . . . . . 47

*Useful Addresses*. . . . . . . . . . . . . . . . . . . . . 47

*Index* . . . . . . . . . . . . . . . . . . . . . . . . . . . . . 48

Some words are shown in bold, **like this.** You can find out what they mean by looking in the glossary.

# What Is a Cockatiel?

If you are reading this book, then probably you or someone you know is thinking about getting a cockatiel. Not only are you considering a great pet, but you have also made a very sensible start by trying to find out as much as you can about cockatiels before you make a decision to get one. Far too many people buy new pets without much idea about how to take care of them, which only ends up making both the owner and the new pet very unhappy.

Cockatiels are a type of parrot. They are closely related to cockatoos, parakeets, and macaws. Cockatiels make very good pets. They are particularly nice pets for children and young adults. They are relatively easy to care for. If you give them the care they need and plenty of love and attention, they can live for about fourteen years.

**This handsome bird shows off the crest of feathers on its head.**

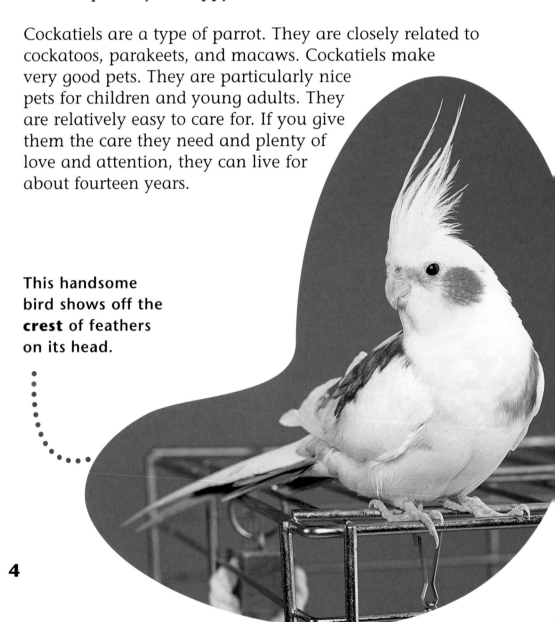

## Where do they come from?

In the wild, cockatiels are very common in Australia, where they can be seen in people's gardens or looking for food at the edge of roadsides. They are smaller than macaws and the larger types of parrots. Cockatiels grow to a length of about 11 inches (28 centimeters), including their long tail.

**These birds are rose-breasted cockatoos. They are closely related to cockatiels.**

## Why are they called cockatiels?

• The name cockatiel comes from the **Portuguese** word *cacathitho*, which means "little cockatoo."

## Special feet

Cockatiels and all parrots have very unusual feet for birds. Most birds have three toes pointing forward and one pointing backward. Cockatiels and other parrots, however, have two toes pointing forward and two pointing backward. This allows them to pick up their food and hold it while they eat, which is particularly common among the larger parrots, although less so with cockatiels.

**5**

## Colors and markings

Cockatiels are beautiful birds, with a **crest** of feathers on the top of their head. They come in a variety of colors and color patterns but are not as brightly colored as parakeets and macaws.

Cockatiels may be any combination of black, red, white, and yellow. A cockatiel may have all these colors or just one or two of them. Some are quite brightly colored, while others are very pale. From time to time, you will find one with no color at all. This is called an **albino.** There are a few common color varieties.

**Many cockatiels have orange cheeks.**

Here are two normal grey cockatiels and a lutino cockatiel perched on a branch. Notice how their toes wrap around the branch.

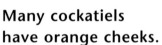

## Some varieties of cockatiel

- Pied cockatiels are blotchy looking with white and yellow patches.
- Pearl cockatiels have white or yellow feathers, and each feather has a gray edge.
- Lutino birds don't have any black coloring. They are pale yellow.
- The normal grey coloring is probably most commonly seen. The bird has a mainly gray body with a yellow head and white bands on the wings.

## Pets are a big responsibility

As with any animal, once you take on the responsibility of owning a pet, you are completely responsible for its care and its behavior. You need to decide if you really can provide all the care that your new pet needs.

You will have to spend time with your pet every day and take care of its needs. If you think that it may be ill, you should always get a vet to check it out.

Cockatiels are intelligent and **sociable** birds. Because of their high intelligence, they need **stimulation** from you and their environment.

## Your responsibilities

- Never buy a pet without first considering the good as well as the bad points.
- Never buy a pet because you feel sorry for it.
- Young children are not allowed to buy pets. Take an adult with you when you buy your cockatiel.
- When you own a pet, it is your duty to care for it, so you need to decide if you really can.
- If your pet is ill, you need to take it to the vet. Make sure you know a good vet before you buy your cockatiel.

# Cockatiels in the Wild

When thinking about getting a pet, it is often a good idea to find out how the animal lives naturally in the wild. This will help you understand the best way to care for your pet.

## Where do they live?

Cockatiels live in the wild in Australia, particularly in the middle of the country, where it is very hot and dry. They like to make their nests in the **hollows** of trees. They try to find trees that are near water so that they don't have to travel far to get a drink. They will normally nest 6.5–26 feet (2–8 meters) off the ground depending on where the suitable hollows are in the tree.

This group of cockatiel chicks has just hatched. Both cockatiel parents prepare the nest hollow, tend the eggs, and care for their young.

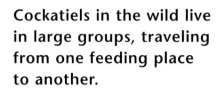

Cockatiels in the wild live in large groups, traveling from one feeding place to another.

## How do they eat?

Cockatiels usually look for their food on the ground, where they eat various grass seeds, as well as shoots and buds of different plants. If they are eating on the ground and are frightened by a **predator,** cockatiels will fly up into the branches of trees. If your pet cockatiel becomes scared, it will automatically fly upward.

## Who do they live with?

Cockatiels are **sociable** birds that live in large flocks. In the wild they have to constantly keep moving in search of water, so it is safer and easier to do this in a large group. They whistle to let other flock members know of danger, food, or their location. Their pale coloring helps **camouflage** them from predators.

Wild cockatiels eat seeds, leaves, bark, fruit, and berries.

# Is a Cockatiel for You?

It is very important to choose a pet that fits in with your way of life and your daily routine, and one that will provide you with all the things that you want from it. Otherwise you will soon get bored, and neither you nor your new pet will be happy.

A cockatiel is an ideal first pet. They are very friendly and intelligent birds that respond well to human contact. They are not very expensive or difficult to care for. But before you make up your mind, here are some points that you should consider.

## Are they good with other pets?

Birds and cats do not get along well together, so if you have a cat it's probably best not to buy a cockatiel. Dogs are not as bad, as long as the bird's cage is well out of the dog's way. The cockatiel should not be let out of its cage when the dog is around. Other pets such as **rodents,** rabbits, and other birds should all be able to live in peace together, as long as they are all housed separately.

Having two pets can be twice as much fun, as long as you get the right combination!

## Can I tame a cockatiel?

Cockatiels are very intelligent and will very quickly learn to sit on your finger and do tricks. They can even be taught to repeat a word or two. Cockatiels are not quite as good at "talking" as some of the larger parrots, but if you are patient, they can learn a few words. The more time you spend with your cockatiel, the **tamer** it will become.

## How much space does a cockatiel need?

Cockatiels need to be able to fly and stretch their wings. A regular parakeet cage is not big enough for a cockatiel. For a single bird, the cage should by at least 24 inches (60 centimeters) by 24 inches (60 centimeters) by 36 inches (90 centimeters).

Once your cockatiel gets familiar with you, it will happily spend a lot of time playing with you.

When choosing a cage for your cockatiel, the bigger the better. Buy the largest one you have space for and can afford.

## A big commitment

Any animal is a big commitment, and you need to make sure that you will be able to give it all the care and attention it needs. A cockatiel will need at least fifteen minutes of care a day and could live for about fourteen years. Can you commit to that amount of time every day for the rest of your pet's life?

## Vacations

You also need to think about who will take care of your pet if you go on vacation. You will need to find someone who is willing to do this for you and whom you trust completely.

## Lots of attention

Other than food and water, the most important thing that you need to give your cockatiel is attention. They need much more company and **stimulation** than other birds. If they don't get the attention they need, they can suffer from a number of illnesses and disorders. They can even die from boredom.

If you are not at home very much, maybe you should consider getting two birds. That way, they will have a friend for company if you are not around. However, they will still need some attention from you.

This bird is cleaning its feathers. This is a healthy habit and cockatiels spend a lot of time doing it.

## Cockatiel good points

- They are easy to **tame**.
- They are less expensive to care for than dogs and cats.
- They are very friendly and intelligent, so they can learn tricks easily.
- They are attractive birds and fun to watch.
- They don't get ill very often.

You will need to clean the floor around and under the cage every day to get rid of droppings and scattered seeds.

## Cockatiel not-so-good points

- They need a lot of attention to keep them from being bored.
- They need a lot of space. A nice big cage can be quite expensive and takes up a lot of room.
- A **hand-reared** bird can be quite expensive.
- You will need someone to look after them when you go away.

# Choosing a Cockatiel

The first thing you need to think about is how many birds you want to have. A single bird is often thought to become **tamer** than a pair, because it will soon consider itself a part of the family it lives with. However, a single bird will need a lot more time and attention to keep it from getting bored. If you think that your new pet will have to be left by itself for several hours a day, then you should consider getting two birds.

Another possibility is to keep an **aviary.** This allows the birds to live in a way that is similar to how they would live in the wild. It allows you to keep several birds at a time. Aviaries also give the birds much more space. Aviary birds will probably not become as tame as single birds or a pair. If this is the first time that you have owned a cockatiel or any birds, it's probably best to get used to keeping just one or a pair before you start to think about setting up an aviary.

If you keep many **species** of birds, make sure that they are suited to living in the same aviary.

## Getting ready

You must get the cage and all the necessary equipment, including food, before you purchase your bird. The stress of being moved will upset the bird, so it needs to be placed quickly in its new cage and environment.

## Pet shop or breeder?

There are good points and bad points about buying your new cockatiel from either a pet shop or a breeder. Some pet shops may offer a written **guarantee**, so if your new pet doesn't seem to be very healthy even after taking it to the vet, you can return the bird and get your money back. Breeders are less likely to do this.

Breeders, however, have a lot more experience **rearing** and caring for cockatiels. They can often offer advice whenever you need it throughout your bird's life. Breeders normally sell **hand-reared** birds which, although more expensive, will ultimately become tamer, friendlier pets. Birds purchased from good breeders will usually have been less exposed to disease, so they are often healthier. They also will not have had to experience the stress of being moved to a pet shop or the noise and hassle of being kept in a shop environment.

Pet shops have a large selection of cages and other equipment you will need. At a pet shop you can buy your cockatiel and everything you need for it.

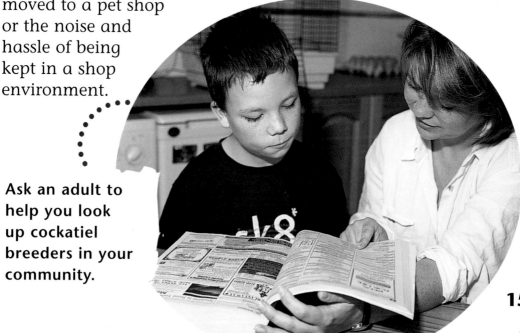

Ask an adult to help you look up cockatiel breeders in your community.

## Male or female?

If you have decided to get just one cockatiel, you need to decide whether to have a male or a female bird. There are slight differences in coloring between the sexes, but not much in terms of **temperament** and intelligence. Both sexes make equally good pets. Obviously, if you buy a male and female pair, they may have babies! So if you are not ready for this, make sure you buy either just one bird or two of the same sex.

## How can you tell?

The **variation** in coloring between the sexes is the easiest way to tell your bird's sex, but such differences are not noticeable until the bird is several months old. If you are getting a young bird, the pet shop or breeder will probably be able to tell you which sex the bird is before you buy it.

Males usually have stronger, brighter colors than females, especially in the cheek patches.

You should have a good look around the shop before you buy your pet.

16

## Hand-reared or not hand-reared?

A **hand-reared** bird is one that has been fed and handled by humans from an early age. Hand-reared birds can be bought from a breeder or from some good pet shops. Hand-reared birds will be quite **tame** right from the start. This will save you the time of having to get them used to human contact. However, hand-reared cockatiels cost more money (maybe three or four times as much) than a bird that was not hand reared. If you are planning to get a young bird and have plenty of time to spend taming it yourself, it won't be long before your new pet is as tame as a hand-reared one.

## Top tip

**Humane societies** sometimes have older birds that are already tame. These birds need a new home, and you can adopt them for a small fee.

These ten-day old chicks are being hand fed by a breeder.

## How will I know if it is healthy?

When you go to choose your new pet, there are a few things that will show you if the bird is healthy and likely to make a good pet.

The first thing to check for is the smell. Although birds will give off a faint bird **aroma,** there shouldn't be any bad smells. It is fine if there are a few droppings on the floor of the cage, but there shouldn't be a thick covering all over the floor and perches. If the breeder or pet shop owner is caring for the birds properly and they are healthy, the cockatiel cages should be reasonably clean and should not smell bad.

Cockatiels sleep when it gets dark, so if you choose your new pet during the day when it is light, the birds should all be awake. They should be eating or flying around. A sleepy bird may take a nap on its perch with one leg tucked up under itself, but it will soon straighten up and open its eyes when you move closer.

## What age?

If you want to **tame** your cockatiel yourself, it is best to get one as soon as it is ready to leave its mother. This will be at around eight to twelve weeks. Older birds will also make excellent pets but will probably take longer to tame.

This is a young cockatiel. It will take less time to become tame.

18

## Watch out

If a bird is sitting with its eyes closed and its feathers all puffed up and does not respond when you get closer, it is probably best to choose another one. A healthy bird will be **alert** and lively. It will be friendly but a bit nervous.

You should also pay attention to the condition of the feathers. Although one or two feathers may have been pulled out during fights with other birds in their cage, a healthy cockatiel will always make sure that its feathers re kept clean.

You should look closely when choosing your bird and compare how it looks with the others in the cage.

## Top tip

It you can get a closer look, make sure that there is no **discharge** coming from the bird's eyes, beak, beak **vents,** or rear end. Avoid a bird with runny eyes, a runny beak, or with droppings stuck around its rear.

**19**

# What Do I Need?

The first thing that you will need to buy before you get your new cockatiel is a nice, large cage. Remember that for a single bird the cage should be at least 24 inches (60 centimeters) by 24 inches (60 centimeters) by 36 inches (90 centimeters). A pair of birds should be given twice as much space. Cockatiels like to climb up and down. In the wild they would naturally spend time on the ground looking for food. Then later they would fly up into the trees. So, if you have the choice, it is better to get a tall cage rather than a wide one of the same size.

Cockatiels enjoy climbing up and down to explore the cage. The bars of the cage should therefore be horizontal so that they can use them as a ladder. You should make sure that the bars of the cage are not more than 1/3 inch (1 centimeter) apart, otherwise your new pet may push its head through the bars and hurt itself.

You should make sure that the cage is made of "chew-proof" materials, because over time your new bird will chew its way through most plastics and wood.

There are plenty of metal cages designed especially for cockatiels that are a good size and made of the right materials.

## Top tip

Some cages, particularly antique ones, come in a wide variety of shapes, metals, and colors, These may look nice, but they can be very dangerous for your cockatiel. The paint used on these cages can be poisonous to birds, so you should avoid these and stick to the ones sold at good pet shops.

## Setting up the cage

Once you have the main cage, you will need to add some perches. It is a good idea to put a few in at different angles and at different heights to mimic the positioning of tree branches in the wild. It is very important to include perches of different thicknesses. This will help exercise the bird's feet by making it grip different-sized bars.

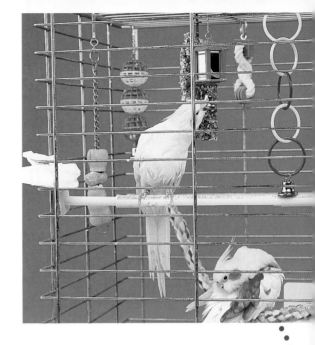

The bottom of the cage should have a lining made especially for bird cages. You can buy these linings at most good pet shops. You can buy sheets of **grit**-covered paper that can be thrown away each day after they become covered in droppings. Or you can use special bird-friendly wood shavings. Using wood shavings makes the cage slightly more difficult to clean out. But you only need to replace the shavings every couple of days.

Always make sure that there is enough room between the perches for your cockatiel to fly and stretch its wings.

**Some cockatiels have a bad reaction to newspaper ink. Check with your vet about the best lining material.**

## Inside or outside?

The "indoor or outdoor" question very much depends on the climate where you live, how much space you have in your home, and how many birds you wish to keep. Usually, a single bird or a pair of birds would be kept in a cage in the house.

**An outside cage or aviary usually allows you to give the birds more space, but it will require a great deal of time and effort to build.**

An outside cage will have to meet a lot of special requirements to ensure that the bird is kept safe, healthy, and happy. Unless you live in a climate where it is warm year round, you should keep your bird's cage inside. This will enable you to spend much more time with them. They will become **tame,** because they will live as part of your family.

## Travel cages

There may come a time when you will need to move your pet from one place to another. For example, you may go on vacation and need to leave your pet with a friend or you may need to take it to the vet. It is a good idea to have a smaller travel cage that you keep for this purpose.

## Toys

Cockatiels are very intelligent birds and need a lot of things to keep them busy and interested. Although toys are no substitute for your company, they will help keep your pet happy and entertained when you have other things to do.

There is a huge variety of toys especially designed for cockatiels and parrots that you can get from most good pet shops. The best ones are those that encourage behavior similar to that of cockatiels in the wild. Toys that allow your pet to climb will be particularly popular, as will toys made from ropes that can be picked at and slowly destroyed! Give your pet plenty of variety to keep it from getting bored.

Some toys can be attached to the side of the cage, while others can be left loose on the bottom.

You could set up the travel cage as a play cage so that your cockatiel will get used to it and won't be scared if it has to be taken somewhere in it.

## Food and water bowls

Most good cages will come with all the necessary bowls and containers for food and water. If not, you can buy them at most pet shops.

Make sure that the bowls are made out of a strong, chew-proof material and that they don't have any sharp edges that could hurt your pet.

## Cuttlebones

A **cuttlebone** is the inside shell of a cuttlefish, a sea animal related to **squids.** You will often see a cuttlebone in bird cages. It is flat, white, and oval shaped. Cuttlebones have two main uses. They are an excellent source of **calcium,** which your bird needs to help keep its bones and feathers healthy. Also, the cuttlebone is very hard. Your cockatiel will chew it, which will help keep its beak in good condition and keep the beak from growing too long.

# Grit

Cockatiels do not eat and **digest** food they same way people do. They do not chew food like we do. They need to swallow little bits of **grit** that stay inside them and help crush up the food they eat. They don't need to swallow a lot of grit, but some should always be available for them. You should replace the grit when it becomes old or covered in droppings, but one small bag will be more than enough to last your bird its whole life.

You can buy special bird grit from most pet shops. Grit should be offered to your bird in a separate container from the food.

This cockatiel is chewing on a cuttlebone. Remember to replace the cuttlebones when they get eaten.

# Caring for Your Cockatiel

Once you have set up the cage with all the correct equipment and bought your new pet, you can start to get to know each other. The best way to do this is to spend as much time with it as possible. Soon you will have settled into a routine that works for both of you and lets you give your cockatiel the best care possible.

## Where should I put the cage?

Since cockatiels are such friendly birds and love plenty of attention, it is best to put the cage in a room that gets used a lot. Although the kitchen may be the busiest room, the cooking smells and sounds may be a bit too much for your new pet. In fact, some smells may even be harmful.

The living room is probably the best place for the cage. If you spend a lot of time in your bedroom, it is a good choice, too.

## Top tip

- You need to make sure that the cage is not in a draft, so do not place it by a door or window.
- It is also best to have the cage raised well above the floor. This will keep your bird out of the way of any other pets and give it a better view of what is going on in the house.

Once your cockatiel becomes tame, you can bring it out of its cage to play with it.

Never leave your pet alone outside because cats or dogs from the neighborhood could come over and scare it.

## Taking your cockatiel outside

Even a very **tame** bird should never be taken outside without being in a cage. The most well-behaved bird can become confused outside, fly off, and be unable to find its way back home. However, your bird will enjoy being taken outside in its cage to get a bit of fresh air and a change of scenery. Make sure that you don't put the cage in direct sunlight. Even if part of the cage is in the sun there should always be a part in the shade, too, where your bird can go if it gets too hot. Never take your pet outside when it is very cold or if it is raining.

## What should I feed my cockatiel?

A cockatiel should be fed about 50 percent cereals, grains, and seeds. About 45 percent of its diet should be fresh vegetables and 5 percent fresh fruit. You can buy premixed bird foods that contain the right balance of cereals, grains, and seeds. These mixes will save you time and effort.

You can then add fresh fruit and vegetables. Cockatiels enjoy oranges, apples, carrots, brussels sprouts, spinach, broccoli, and dandelion greens. A small slice of apple and a small sprout, for example, will be plenty for one day. Don't give your pet much more than this, or it may get **diarrhea.**

There are many different varieties of bird food available at pet shops, so always read the labels to make sure they are suitable for cockatiels.

## Top tips

- You should always throw away any fresh food that is not eaten within one day. Any uneaten seeds can be left for a couple of days before you throw them out.
- Water should be replaced every day.

## New food

If you introduce new foods to your cockatiel, take special notice of your bird's health. If your pet starts breathing heavily, drinking a lot of water, or if its droppings become runny, it could be having a bad reaction to the food. You should stop feeding it the new food at once.

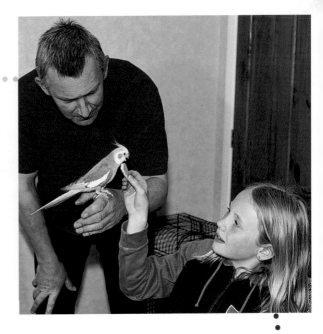

Be careful when you feed your pet new food.

## Illness and injury

Cockatiels do not often become sick or injured, but it can happen. Watch how your pet normally looks and behaves so that you will be able to notice right away if it starts behaving differently or showing signs of illness or injury. If you think that your cockatiel may be sick or injured, it is best to take it to the veterinarian.

Always remember to wash your hands before and after you handle your bird or the cage.

## Cleaning out the cage

In addition to the daily and weekly jobs of cleaning the floor of the cage and the perches and toys, the whole cage should be cleaned out completely at least once a month. It is best to do this with a helper. One person can clean the cage, and the other can play with the bird or supervise it while it flies around the room.

## Getting into a routine

It is a good idea with any pet to get into a routine that suits you. If you always get up at 8:00 a.m. but are too rushed and tired to spend time with your pet, get it used to being given just a small bit of food at this time. When you get home in the evening and have more time to spend with your pet, you can give it a larger meal, clean out the cage, and play with it. It will soon get used to this routine and will be ready and waiting for you in the evening, knowing that this is when you will spend time with it.

## Top tip

If your bird is not very **tame** or if you don't have anyone to help you, you should buy a second cage that your bird can wait in while you clean its main cage. Putting some special toys in the spare cage will help keep your bird happy and entertained.

Don't forget to clean under the cage, too. Cockatiels can be very messy!

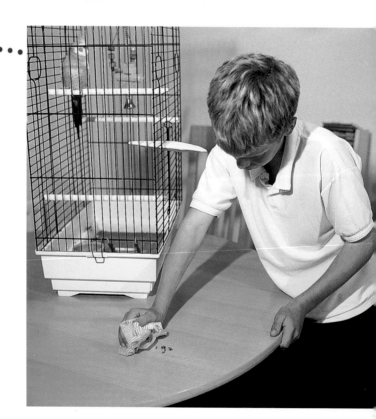

30

# Daily, weekly, and monthly tasks

**Every day you should:**

- Give your pet fresh food and water.
- Throw away any uneaten food from the day before.
- Change the lining of the cage.
- Give your pet plenty of exercise flying around the room (as long as it is safe to do so).
- Spend as much time playing with your pet as possible.

**Once a week you should:**

- Clean the perches, toys, and bowls.
- Give your pet a bath. (see page 36).

**Once a month you should:**

- Clean out the whole cage with a good pet cage disinfectant.

## Spending time with your cockatiel

A tame cockatiel will be unhappy if you leave it on its own for more than about eight hours a day. Leaving the TV or radio on will help keep your pet happy, but this can't be done every day. You should try to spend at least an hour a day playing and talking with your pet. The rest of the time it should be able to **interact** with your family, watching you all go about your daily tasks.

**Placing a mirror in the cage will also help keep your pet occupied.**

# Can We Make Friends?

A single cockatiel kept as a pet will be a lot easier to **tame** than a pair of cockatiels or a whole **aviary** full. Getting a **hand-reared** bird will also make the taming process a lot easier. The main thing to remember is that the more time you spend with your cockatiel, the tamer it will become.

Once you bring your new pet home, you should give it a few hours of peace and quiet. Doing this will help it settle into its new home. You will probably be very excited and eager to start getting to know your new cockatiel as soon as possible, but your pet will be quite nervous at first. Give it some time alone before you start.

## Winning your cockatiel's trust

Once your cockatiel gets used to its new cage, you could start by giving it a tasty treat through the bars of the cage. You might try a bit of cabbage or apple. While you offer the treat, speak to it in a gentle, quiet voice. Once it is ready to take the food from your fingers, you can put your hand in the cage to offer the treats. It may be a few days before you can do this.

Eventually, your new pet will happily come and sit on your finger as soon as you put your hand inside the cage.

Be very patient when you are first making friends with your new pet.

## Out of the cage

If the room is safe and all doors and windows are closed, you can gently bring your finger, with your bird perched on it, out of the cage.

It will take a while to build the relationship between you and your cockatiel. But cockatiels are quick learners, and if you spend enough time with them, (especially in the first few months) they will become very tame.

If you press your finger gently on your cockatiel's chest, as if offering it as a perch, your bird will naturally climb up on it. This is how you can return your tame cockatiel to its cage once its playtime is over.

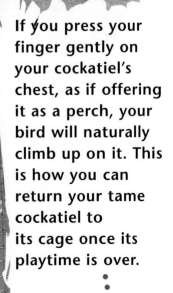

# Fun Time Together

Because cockatiels are so intelligent and eager to learn, they can quite easily be taught to do simple tricks. Putting a coin in a purse or a toy in a toy box are the types of tricks that your cockatiel can quickly learn to do.

The easiest way to teach your cockatiel this type of trick is with **bribery!** If you put a shiny new coin on the table in front of your bird it should naturally pick it up out of curiosity to see what it is. You should then give your bird a little treat such as slice of apple or a piece of cabbage.

Next time, offer the treat after the coin is picked up but from a little distance away. Make the bird walk a few steps to get the treat. Once it gets to the treat still carrying the coin, you can give it the treat. Continue to do this in stages until the bird understands that it only gets the treat if it picks up the coin and carries it to you. You can then introduce the purse and follow the same steps.

**Once your cockatiel is tame, you can teach it tricks!**

34

This is the basic way to teach a cockatiel to do things, slowly and in simple stages. You can be as imaginative as you like and teach your cockatiel to do all sorts of entertaining tricks, which will be great fun for you and your pet.

## An adventure playground

Cockatiels love to climb and explore, and they love nothing better than to be let loose on an interesting selection of safe, objects they can chew! They will have fun playing with old paper-towel tubes, cardboard boxes (without any print), ropes, and other similar things. You can really use your imagination and create a fantastic adventure playground for your pet. You will have a lot of fun building it, and your cockatiel will have hours of pleasure destroying it!

### Top tip

Make sure that the adventure playground is set up in a safe place. Never leave your bird alone when it is out of its cage. Even seemingly safe places can have hidden dangers for your pet.

Ladders, swings, and climbing frames will keep your cockatiel entertained.

## Having a bath

Cockatiels enjoy baths. You can give your pet a bath in a large shallow dish. Put enough clean water in the dish to just cover the bottom. When letting your bird take a bath, make sure you supervise it the entire time it is in the water. It could drown if you leave it alone. Don't leave the dish of water in the cage. Remove it when your bird has finished.

The other way of cleaning your cockatiel is to spray it with water from a clean household-plant spray bottle.

**Always make sure that the spray bottle is completely clean and has never contained any chemicals that may be harmful to your bird.**

**You can give your bird a bath in a custom-made cockatiel bathtub!**

## Catching a cold

Never leave a wet cockatiel outside or in a draft, because it will easily catch a cold. After your cockatiel has washed, make sure there is somewhere warm where it can sit to dry off. Never dry it with a hair dryer!

## Teaching your cockatiel to talk

Cockatiels are not great talkers in comparison to parakeets and some of the larger parrots. However, if you have the patience, a cockatiel should be able to learn a few words. You should repeat the same word over and over again with a little gap in between. Use the same tone of voice every time you say the word. Don't try anything too difficult at first. Start with its name or "hello." Once the bird has learned one or two simple words, you can move on to other slightly longer phrases. **Bribery** will work here, too, so always keep a tasty bit of apple ready to reward your bird if it says things correctly.

Each bird's talking ability is different. Some may never say a word despite hours of teaching. But if your bird do learn to say a few things, it is well worth the effort.

**Cockatiels may not be great talkers, but they are certainly great companions.**

37

# Keeping Your Cockatiel Healthy

Cockatiels are usually very healthy birds and don't often become sick. The best way to keep them healthy is to make sure they are well cared for.

Drafts are one of the main causes of illness in cockatiels. Cockatiels can catch a cold very easily, so to keep your pet healthy, keep it out of drafts. Boredom is the other main problem and can lead to the death of a bird. If you keep your cockatiel in a draft-free, warm, dry, clean environment in a large cage, give it fresh food and water every day, and spend as much time with it as possible, you should have a very healthy bird.

## New bird

The only other situation that possibly could be dangerous for your pet is if a new bird is introduced to either a single bird or an **aviary.** The new bird could bring with it a number of diseases, because you will not be sure if it is completely healthy when you buy it. If you have decided to buy a second bird to keep your single bird company or if you wish to add another to your aviary, you must keep it in a separate place until you have had it checked by a veterinarian.

After you have had the new bird checked by the vet, you can put it in with the others and watch it make friends.

# Wing, beak, and claw clipping

Wing clipping is a difficult subject. Some people like to do it, and others are strongly against it. A bird that has had its wings clipped has had some of the wing feathers cut so that the bird cannot fly away. This sometimes makes **taming** the bird easier. If you wish to have your bird's wings clipped, you should take it to a vet. Never try to do it yourself, because you could end up hurting your bird very badly.

Beak and claw clipping, however, are done to help improve your bird's health and quality of life. Beak clipping may need to be done in birds in which the beak has grown too long. This can keep the bird from eating properly. Claws will need to be clipped if they become too long and are making it difficult for your bird to walk and hold on to its perches. However, never try to clip the beak or claws yourself, because you can easily hurt your pet.

If you think that your bird's claws or beak have become too long, you should take it to a vet who will be able to clip them for you.

# Some Health Problems

In the wild, birds that become ill will usually try to pretend that they are not sick. They do not want to seem ill, because this will attract the attention of **predators** who would see them as easy **prey.** Cockatiels that are kept as pets will also often hide the fact that they are not feeling well, which makes it difficult for you to tell if they are sick.

A sick cockatiel will usually sit on the ground or at the end of a perch with its feathers all puffed up, eyes closed, and its head tucked back. It won't seem very **alert** even if you talk to it and will generally not seem like its normal self.

Other signs of illness or injury include runny droppings, runny eyes, and a runny beak or beak **vents.** Breathing problems, messy feathers, a dirty rear end, and a lack of interest also usually mean your pet is ill. If you think that your cockatiel is sick or injured, take it to the vet at once.

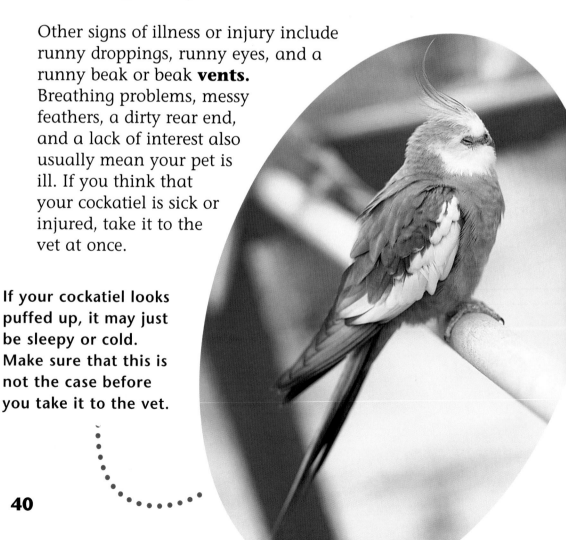

**If your cockatiel looks puffed up, it may just be sleepy or cold. Make sure that this is not the case before you take it to the vet.**

## Colds

Cockatiels should never be kept near a window or a door because drafts can easily cause breathing problems and colds. If your bird starts to make wheezing noises and looks as if it is having trouble breathing, you should keep it separate from any other birds and get it to a vet as soon as possible.

This is what healthy cockatiel droppings should look like.

## Burns

Cockatiels don't know if something is going to be hot. If you let your bird fly into the kitchen and an electric burner is on, your bird will only see it as a nice flat landing surface and will get bad burns on its feet.

## Drowning

One fairly common cause of death in **tame** cockatiels is drowning. Half-full glasses of water look very appealing to a cockatiel, but the bird can easily fall in and get stuck head down in the liquid. It can drown in seconds.

## Boredom

It is important not to let your cockatiel get bored. This is the most common cause of death in all parrots. If you do not think you will be able to give your bird the attention it needs, either find it a new home or get another cockatiel to keep it company.

A cockatiel should never be left alone with no company or toys to keep it busy.

41

# When a Cockatiel Dies

Sadly, the time will come when your pet will die. This is obviously a very natural thing, and there is nothing that you can do to keep it from happening. It doesn't matter how well you look after your pet, one day it will just be time for it to go. Sometimes this will happen without warning and you may discover your pet has passed away during the night. Other times you may be aware that your pet is sick or old. The vet may tell you that it will die very soon.

**If your cockatiel is too ill or old to enjoy its life, you and your vet may decide to put it to sleep.**

## Putting your pet to sleep

Sometimes you and your vet may feel that a sick or very old cockatiel is no longer enjoying its life and that the kindest think to do for it would be to "put it to sleep." The vet will simply give your pet a little injection, which won't hurt it at all. It will very quickly fall into a deep sleep, and its heart will stop. It won't feel any pain, and it will all be over very quickly. It is a very difficult decision to make, but it is also a very brave one and shows that you are doing the best thing for your pet.

## Feeling sad

When a pet you love dies, it is a very difficult and sad time. It is important to understand that your pet didn't suffer in any way and that it died peacefully after a happy life. Death is just one of those things that happens, and it is not your fault in any way.

It is normal for both children and adults to cry when a loved pet dies or when we think about a pet that has died. After a while the sadness will pass and you can just remember the good times that you had with your pet.

You can decorate the grave with flowers so that your pet's resting place looks very special.

# Keeping a Record

Just like any friend or member of your family, your pet should have a place in your photo album or even an album all of its own. It is fun to create such an album and after your pet has died, it will give you something to remember it by.

It is also a nice idea to make notes about your cockatiel, such as when you first brought it home and how you **tamed** it. You could keep a diary of all the things you did with your pet and the progress it made as you tamed it and taught it new tricks.

Take photos of your bird with different members of your family and with friends that visit. You may want to create a "hall of fame" with all the people that your bird has played with. You can also take some pictures of your bird doing its favorite tricks and eating its favorite food. You could then make up funny captions to go with your pictures and make them into a comic book about your pet.

**You can have great fun taking pictures of your cockatiel doing all the things that you both enjoy.**

## A special diary

You may want to keep a scrapbook full of articles and photos you clip from magazines about cockatiels and other parrots. You can really be creative, decorating it with lots of pictures. Include some of your own drawings, too. You could even write your own book about keeping and caring for cockatiels!

## Top tip

You can start your scrapbook with the first day you saw your pet and then go on to show how your friendship grew!

A scrapbook is a great way to record your pet's life, and it will stay with you for years after you've said good-bye to your pet.

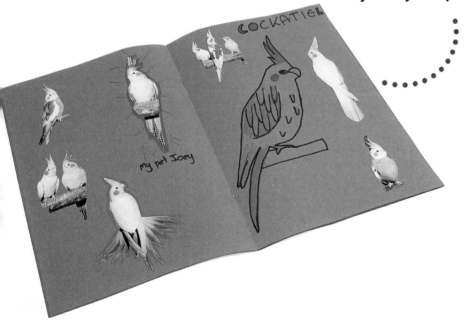

# Glossary

**albino**  animal that has no coloring

**alert**  aware of what is going on

**aroma**  smell

**aviary**  large bird cage that is usually outside

**bribery**  offering something in return for something else

**calcium**  element found in some foods that helps keep bones healthy

**camouflage**  blend in with surroundings

**crest**  tuft of feathers on the head of a bird

**cuttlebone**  inside shell of a squidlike creature known as a cuttlefish

**diarrhea**  runny droppings

**digest**  break down food so it can be absorbed

**discharge**  oozing liquid

**grit**  very small bits of stone

**guarantee**  promise that what is purchased is of good quality

**hand-reared**  describes a bird that has been fed and handled by humans from an early age

**hollow**  hole

**humane society**  place in which animals without a home live and may be adopted

**interact**  talk to or play with

**Portuguese**  coming from Portugal

**predator**  animal that hunts and kills other animals for food

**prey**  animal that is eaten by another animal

**rear**  feed and care for a baby animal and help it grow and develop

**rodent**  small animal with two long front teeth. Mice and rats are rodents.

**sociable**  enjoying contact with others

**species**  group of animals that have the same features and can have babies with each other

**squid**  soft-bodied sea creature with eight arms and two tentacles

**stimulation**  something that sparks interest

**tame**  used to being with people

**temperament**  way an animal usually acts. For example, a cockatiel might have a friendly temperament or a nervous temperament.

**variation**  difference

**vent**  hole in a cockatiel's beak

# Further Reading

Grindol, Diane. *The Complete Book of Cockatiels*. Hoboken, N.J.: Howell Book House, 1998.

Moustaki, Nikki. *Why Do Cockatiels Do That?* Irvine, Calif.: Bowtie Press, 2003.

Viner, B. Bradley. *All About Your Cockatiel*. Hauppauge, N.Y.: Barron's Educational Series, 1999.

Zeaman, John. *Exotic Pets: From Alligators to Zebra Fish*. Danbury, Conn.: Franklin Watts, 1999.

# Useful Addresses

The American Society for the Prevention of Cruelty to Animals
424 E. 92nd St.
New York, NY 10128
Tel: (212) 876-7700
http://www.aspca.org

National Alternative Pet Association
P.O. Box 369
Burnet, TX 78611
http://www.altpet.net

The National Cockatiel Society
Secretary: Nancy Rocheleau
1828 Stovall St.
Bullhead City, AZ 86443
Tel: (928) 704-2883
http://www.cockatiels.org

**Disclaimer**
All Internet addresses (URLs) given in this book were valid at the time of going to press. However, due to the dynamic nature of the Internet, some addresses may have changed, or sites may have ceased to exist since publication. While the author and publisher regret any inconveniences this may cause readers, no responsibility for any such changes can be accepted by either the author or the publisher.

# Index

adventure playground 35
albinos 6
attention and stimulation 4, 12, 13, 14, 23, 26, 31, 41
aviary 14, 22, 38

bathing your cockatiel 36, 37
beak 19, 24, 40
beak and claw clipping 39
boredom 12, 13, 14, 38, 41
breeders 15, 16, 17
burns 41

cage 11, 13, 15, 20–25, 26, 27, 30, 33
cage cleaning 21, 29, 30, 31
cage liners 21
cage, outdoor 22
calcium 24
choosing your cockatiel 7, 14–19
claws 39
colds 37, 38, 41
colors and patterns 6, 9, 16
crest 4, 6
cuttlebones 24, 25

death 12, 38, 41, 42–43
diarrhea 28
drafts 26, 38, 41
droppings 18, 19, 29, 40
drowning 36, 41

exercise 21, 31
eyes, runny 19, 40

feathers 6, 19, 24, 40
feet and toes 5, 21
female birds 16
flying 9, 11, 21, 31, 39
food and water 9, 28–29, 31
food and water bowls 24

grit 21, 25

hand-reared birds 15, 17, 32
health 15, 18–19, 38–41
humane societies 17
hygiene 29

illness and injury 12, 28, 29, 38, 40–41
intelligence 10, 11, 13, 16, 23, 34

keeping more than one cockatiel 12, 14, 16, 20, 22, 38, 41

life span 4, 12
lutino cockatiels 6

male birds 16

nests 8
normal grey cockatiels 6

outdoor cage 22
outside, taking your bird 27

parrots 4, 5, 37, 41
pearl cockatiels 6
perches 21
pet shops 15, 16, 17
pets, other 10, 26
pied cockatiels 6
pluses and minuses of cockatiels 13

record book and scrapbook 44–45
routine 30–31

size 5
sleeping 18

"talking" 11, 37
taming and training your cockatiel 11, 14, 15, 17, 18, 22, 32–35, 37, 39
toys 23, 30, 35
travel cage 22, 23
tricks 11, 13, 34–35

vacation care 12, 13
veterinary care 7, 29, 39, 42

wild cockatiels 5, 8–9
wing clipping 39